SHORT SALES AND MANIPILATION OF SECURITIES

COMPILED BY

FRANK FAYANT

NEW YORK

1913

SHORT SALES AND MANIPULATION.

That speculation in securities and commodities, as conducted on the leading Exchanges of the world, is not only a necessary part of the machinery of modern production, but of great benefit to humanity, has been recognized for more than a century by all the leading economists of the universities, as well as by government commissions and the highest courts. (See the collection of opinions by economists, commissions and courts in "Some Thoughts on Speculation" [New York, 1909; privately printed.]

The evils of speculation have resulted in periodic demands for government investigation and restrictive legislation. All government inquiries into speculation have reached the same conclusion—that speculation is economically necessary, and that any radically restrictive legislation must work more harm than good.

The following reports are of especial interest:

> Parliamentary Commission on the London Stock Exchange: 1878.
>
> French Government Commission on the Paris Bourse: 1882.
>
> German Bourse Commission: 1894.
>
> United States Industrial Commission: 1902.
>
> Report on the United States Commission of Corporations on Cotton Exchanges: 1909.
>
> New York State Commission on Speculation: 1909.

Short sales of securities and commodities in the speculative markets are recognized by all the authorities (economists, commissions and courts of the United States, England, France and Germany) as of vital economic importance in modern production.

The manipulation of the speculative markets is likewise recognized as a necessary and useful part of the machinery of speculation, when it is honestly done. But dishonest manipulation of the markets is universally condemned, just as any other dishonest manipulation in business.

Dishonest manipulation is not only punishable under the common law, but is punishable under the rules of the leading exchanges.

OPINIONS ON SHORT SALES AND MANIPULATION.

I. Particularly on Short Sales.

The New York State Commission on Speculation (1909) reported to Governor Hughes on the question of short selling as follows:

> We have been strongly urged to advise the prohibition or limitation of short sales, not only on the theory that it is wrong to agree to sell what one does not possess, but that such sales reduce the market price of the securities involved. We do not think that it is wrong to agree to sell something that one does not now possess, but expects to obtain later.
>
> Contracts and agreement to sell, and deliver in the future, property which one does not possess at the time of the contract, are common in all kinds of business. The man who has "sold short" must some day buy in order to return the stock which he has borrowed to make the short sale. Short-sellers endeavor to select times when prices seem high in order to sell, and times when prices seem low in order to buy, their action in both cases serving to lessen advances and diminish declines of price. In other words, short-selling tends to produce steadiness in prices, which is an advantage to the community. No other means of restraining unwarranted marking up and down of prices has been suggested to us.
>
> The legislation of the State of New York on the subject of short-selling is significant. In 1812 the Legislature passed a law declaring all contracts for the sale of stocks and bonds void, unless the seller at the

time was the actual owner or assignee thereof or authorized by such owner or assignee to sell the same. In 1858 this act was repealed by a statute now in force.

It has been urged that this statute "specifically legalizes stock gambling." As a matter of fact, however, the law would be precisely the same if that statute were repealed, for it is the well settled common law of this country, as established by the decisions of the Supreme Court of the United States and of the State courts, that all contracts, other than mere wagering contracts, for the future purchase or sale of securities or commodities are valid, whether the vendor is, or is not, at the time of making such contract, the owner or possessor of the securities or commodities involved, in the absence of a statute making such contracts illegal. So far as any of these transactions are mere wagering transactions, they are illegal, and not enforceable as the law now stands.

It has been suggested to us that there should be a requirement either by law or by rule of the Stock Exchange, that no one should sell any security without identifying it by number or otherwise. Such a rule would cause great practical difficulties in the case of securities not present in New York at the time when the owner desires to sell them and would increase the labor and cost of doing business. But, even if this were not the effect, the plan contemplates a restriction upon short sales, which, for the reasons set forth above, seems to us undesirable.

It is true that this identification plan exists in England as to sales of bank shares (Leeman Act of 1867); but it has proved a dead letter. It has also been used in times of apprehended panic upon the French Bourse, but opinions in regard to its effect there are conflicting. While some contend that it has been useful in preventing panics, others affirm that it has been used simply for the purpose of protecting bankers who were loaded down with certain securities which they were trying to distribute, and who, through political influence procured the adoption of the rule for their special benefit.

———————

Horace White, Chairman of the Hughes Commission, in the *Journal of Political Economy* (October, 1909), discusses short selling:

Each fall in prices brings in buyers whose purchases minimize the decline, and each rise opens the door for sellers whose sales minimize the advance. In both cases short sellers play a useful part, helping to lessen the advance in the latter case and (by covering) to lessen the decline in the former.

The selling of property for future delivery, by persons who do not immediately possess it, is believed by many to depress prices artifically, to the disadvantage of the producer. This is a fallacy, since every sale requires a purchase of equal magnitude. Nevertheless, it is a constantly recurring fallacy, and it is proper to notice it here.

A manufacturer of cotton goods, for example, in order to keep his mill running all the year round, must make contracts ahead for his material, before the crop of any particular year is picked. The cotton must be of a particular grade. He wishes to be insured against fluctuations in both price and quality; for such insurance he can afford to pay. In fact, he cannot afford to be without it.

There are also men in the cotton trade, of large capital and experience, who keep themselves informed of all the facts touching the crops and the demand and supply of cotton in the world and who find their profit in making contracts for its future delivery. They do not possess the article when they sell it. To them the contract is a matter of speculation and short selling, but it is a perfectly legitimate transaction. To the manufacturer it is virtually a policy of insurance. It enables him to keep his mill running and his hands employed, regardless of bad weather or insect pests or other uncertainties. The same principles apply to the miller who wants wheat, to the distiller, the cattle-feeder, and the starch-maker who want corn, to the brewer who wants hops and barley, to the brassfounder who wants copper, and so on indefinitely.

Insurance is one of two redeeming features of such speculation; and the other, which is even more important, is the steadying effect which it has on market prices. If no speculative buying of produce ever took place, it would be impossible for a grower of wheat or cotton to realize a fair price at once on his entire crop. He would have to deal it out little by little to merchants who, in turn, would pass it on, in the same piecemeal way, to consumers. It is speculative buying which not only enables farmers to realize on their entire crops as soon as they are harvested, but enables them to do so with no disastrous sacrifice of price. When buyers who have future sales in view compete actively with each other, farmers get fair prices for their produce.

Maurice L. Muhleman, who was Secretary of the Hughes Commission, says on short sales (New York *Independent,* Dec. 26, 1912):

Many persons are of the opinion that "short selling," which means that at the moment of sale of a security the seller is not in actual possession thereof, is a vicious practice that should be forbidden. This view is erroneous, as is shown by the circumstance that in the many cases here and abroad where laws were passed to prohibit such sales it was found desirable to repeal them soon afterward. New York's attempt took place in 1812.

There is no device so serviceable to check an unconscionable inflation of prices. The short seller in effect believes that prices are inflated, that they will fall later on, and that they should fall. He therefore undertakes to check the upward tendency by selling, and if sales are sufficiently numerous the inflation is checked. If his opinion is well founded he gains by the transaction to the extent of the difference in prices; but he also serves a useful purpose by preventing the catastrophe which would certainly ensue if prices were "boosted" so high as to bring into the market a large number of shares for sale and cause violent declines, which always breed trouble.

Moreover, under the rules of the Exchange, one who sells shares must actually deliver on the following day, and for this purpose he must borrow the shares until such time as he concludes to buy; that is, when the price has fallen to the figure which he expected. Every short sale must be "covered" by such a purchase at some future date, which has the effect of checking an inordinate fall.

It is ordinarily only the experienced speculator who sells short; the public at large and the small-margin speculators do so rather sparingly because the device appears complicated; hence the great loss waste is not attributable directly to this practice, altho a "bear market" unquestionably causes the "wiping out" of a lot of small-margined operators.

That the device is at times misused must be admitted. A group of speculators, well provided with borrowing power at the banks, may proceed to depress prices by short selling, may buy in shares at the low figures which they create, merely for the purpose of selling them again to the "dear public" at higher prices which they in turn create by reversing their action. When such operations are undertaken purely for the profit to be gained, which, of course, does occur, the "high standards" are evidently strained; but it is to be said that the active Exchange members are not always, and in many cases not at all, responsible for such operations, which are engineered by men outside or by inactive members, the active members serving only as brokers.

In order that a short-selling movement may be successful, it is usually necessary that certain conditions exist; for example, that prices are inflated or that the business outlook is doubtful either in general or as to the particular securities to be sold. Short selling is after all an expression of a kind of pessimism which cannot make much headway in the face of general optimism. Hence, short sellers quite often lose when their judgment is at fault.

Dr. S. S. Huebner (Professor of Commerce in the University of Pennsylvania), in "Scope and Functions of the Stock Market" (*Annals of the American Academy;* May, 1910), page 15:

In this connection attention should be called to the operations of the so-called "bears" who speculate for the fall of stocks though the process of selling "short" that which they do not possess, with the object of buying back later at a lower price, and fulfilling delivery on their contract. Many condemn and few sympathize with the "bear" in the market, because of the belief that it is wrong to sell that which one does not possess, that no economic good is performed by this practice, and that "short selling" artificially depresses security prices. In fact many have recently strongly urged the prohibition of such sales.

A moment's reflection, however, will show that all these conclusions have little basis in fact. These critics forget that "short" selling is a common practice in practically all kinds of business. The manufacturer is expected by the wholesaler to sell his finished wares at a definite price for some definite future delivery, and to insure the delivery of his goods at a stipulated price and time; the manufacturer expects the commission man or produce broker to sell the raw cotton or grain or metal for future delivery at a definite price, long before the crop has beeen harvested or the metal obtained. Contractors, likewise, in contracting for work at a definite price, are constantly selling labor and materials short. The general practice of "hedging" on our exchanges, resorted to by nearly all busiess men handleing our imịportant staples, must necessarily involve a a short sale. In business generally, "short selling" is regarded as a necessary means of insurance against business or speculative losses. If recognized here by all persons who have an understanding of business methods, it certainly cannot be maintained that it is wrong in the stock market to sell something which one does not now possess and intends to buy later.

As regards the two other contentions, that short selling does not perform an economic good, and that it actually depresses the prices of securities, these critics are in the wrong. The short seller in the stock market is often the greatest benefactor in repressing rampant speculative enthusiasm on the one hand, and in checking the effects on security prices of excessive pessimism on the other. "Short sellers" do not determine prices. By selling they simply express their judgment as to what prices will be in the future. If their judgment is wrong they will suffer the penalty of being obliged to go into the market and buy the securities at higher prices. Nine-tenths of the people are by nature "bulls," and the higher prices go, the more optimistic and elated they become. If it were not for a group of "short sellers," who resist an excessive inflation, it would be much easier than now to raise prices through the roof; and then when the inflation became apparent to all, the descent would be abrupt and likely unchecked until the basement was reached. The operations of tht "bear," however, make excessive inflation extremely expensive, and similarly tend to prevent a violent smash, because the "bear," to realize his profits, must become a buyer.

The writer has been told by several members of the New York Stock Exchange that they have seen days of panic when practically the only buyers, who were taking the vast volume of securities dumped on the exchange, were those who had sold "short," and who now turned buyers as the only way of closing their transactions. They were curious to know what would have happened in these panic days, when everybody wished to sell and few cared to invest, if the buying power had depended solely upon the real investment demand of the outside public.

In reply also to the prevalent opinion that "short selling" unduly depresses security values, it should be stated that "short sellers" are frequently the most powerful support which the market possesses. It is an ordinary affair to read in the press that the market is sustained or "put up" at the expense of the "shorts" who, having contracted to deliver at a certain price can frequently easily be driven to "cover." Short selling is thus a beneficial factor in steadying prices and obviating extreme fluctuations. Largely through its action, the discounting of serious depressions does not take the form of a sudden shock or convulsion, but, instead, is spread out over a period of time, giving the actual holder of securities ample time to observe the situation and limit his loss before ruin results. In fact, there did not exist two sides, the "bull" and the "bear." The constant contest between their judgments is sure to give a much saner and truer level of prices than could otherwise exist. "No other means," reports the Hughes' Committee, "of restraining unwarranted marking up and down of prices has been suggested to us."

Henry Crosby Emery (Professor of Political Economy in Yale University) in an article on "Should Speculation be regulated by Law," in the *Journal of Accountancy* (April, 1908), discusses short selling:

It should hardly be necessary to prove that short selling is an entirely honorable and absolutely necessary practice. It is strange, however, that even in fairly intelligent publications we should so frequently see the statement that "it is wrong to sell something that the seller does not own." As a matter of fact it is a most common practice in all lines of business. The manufacturer sells goods before he has produced them, the builder contracts to deliver a house at a certain date which he not only does not possess but for which he has not even bought the raw materials or hired the labor.

If contracts for future delivery were to be limited in all cases to delivery of things already in possession of the contracting party, business would be hampered in a thousand different ways. Furthermore, the very advantages of a speculative market require short selling as an essential feature of the machinery of a continuous market. If there was no bear element in the market to offset the bull element none of the beneficial effects of speculation on prices could be secured. Contrast, for instance, real estate speculation in securities and commodities. In the case of land speculation there can be no short selling because each piece of real estate has a separate character. Consequently we see again and again the evils which result from an entirely uncontrolled land boom sending prices to an absurd point, followed by a sudden and immediate collapse at the end of which prices go down without limit. In the case of organized speculation with short selling, however, this is impossible. Before boom prices get too high the short seller is active in making sales which check the advance, and when a slump comes these same men support the market by their covering transactions.

The short seller is not only a justifiable figure in the speculative market but an absolutely essential one.

Richard T. Ely (Professor of Political Economy in the University of Wisconsin), in "Outlines of Economics" (1910); p. 547.

It is very plain that the fictitious market may be artificially influenced by speculative deals, but as a general thing the fictitious market is ruled by the actual market, not vice versa; and the only influence exerted by gambling in futures upon "spot" prices (with which alone the farmer is concerned) is a good influence. This influence arises out of the effect of future transactions in equalizing consumption and in modifing present use by anticipating future necessity. And the complaint that it requires less capital to "bear" the market than to "bull" it, as well as a great number of ingenious criticisms of a similar kind, would all be negatived—if they were true—by the inevitable consequence that any permanent factor of this kind would be quickly appreciated by speculators and fully discounted. In no market are influences of this kind so accurately detected and so quickly dissipated by competitive forces as the produce and cotton exchanges.

Charles A. Conant, in "The Principles of Banking" (1908); p. 311.

The opportunity of selling products and securities in anticipation of future delivery operates as a form of insurance and diminishes the speculative element in transactions instead of increasing it. The manufacturer, by making contracts for the delivery of his goods at fixed prices, is able to calculate with some degree of certainty upon the relation of the amount realized to the cost of his raw materials, and to manufacture goods upon a scale which would not be possible if he trusted to the accidents of the market at the moment when his products might be finished.

The broker who has a new security which he desires to place from time to time in the future, making possible for instance, the opening of a new country to railway traffic, protects himself against loss resulting from future changes in market conditions by selling other securities for future delivery at current prices. These securities will realize a profit when the date arrives for delivery if the market has in the meantime become unfavorable, and will offset the loss upon his new securities. They will have to be bought at a loss if the movement of prices has been upward, but the upward movement will afford a profit upon the new securities which he is seeking to place upon the market.

II. Particularly on Manipulation.

The Hughes Commission reported on the matter of manipulation as follows:

A subject to which we have devoted much time and thought is that of the manipulation of prices by large interests. This falls into two general classes:

(1) That which is resorted to for the purpose of making a market for issues of new securities.

(2) That which is designed to serve merely speculative purposes in the endeavor to make a profit as the result of fluctuations which have been planned in advance.

The first kind of manipulation has certain advantages, and when not accompanied by "matched orders" is unobjectionable *per se*. It is essential to the organization and carrying through of important enterprises, such as large corporations, that the organizers should be able to raise the money necessary to complete them. This can be done only by the sale of securities. Large blocks of securities, such as are frequently issued by railroad and other companies, cannot be sold over the counter or directly to the ultimate investor, whose confidence in them can, as a rule, be only gradually established. They must therefore, if sold at all, be disposed of to some syndicate, who will in turn pass them on to middlemen or speculators, until, in the course of time, they find their way into the boxes of investors. But prudent investors are not likely to be induced to buy securities which are not regularly quoted on some exchange, and which they cannot sell, or on which they cannot borrow money at their pleasure. If the securities are really good and bids and offers bona fide, open to all sellers and buyers, the operation is harmless. It is merely a method of bringing new investments into public notice.

The second kind of manipulation mentioned is undoubtedly open to serious criticism. It has for its object either the creation of high prices for particular stocks, in order to draw in the public as buyers and to unload upon them the holdings of the operators, or to depress the prices and induce the public to sell. There have been instances of gross and unjustifiable manipulation of securities, as in the case of American Ice stock.

While we have been unable to discover any complete remedy short of abolishing the Stock Exchange itself, we are convinced that the Exchange can prevent the worst forms of this evil by exercising its influence and authority over the members to prevent them. When continued manipulation exists it is patent to experienced observers.

In the foregoing discussion we have confined ourselves to bona fide sales. So far as manipulation of either class is based upon fictitious or so-called "wash sales," it is open to the severest condemnation, and should be prevented by all possible means. These fictitious sales are forbidden by the rules of all the regular exchanges, and are not enforceable at law. They are less frequent than many persons suppose. A transaction must take place upon the floor of the Exchange to be reported, and if not reported does not serve the purpose of those who engage in it. If it takes place on the floor of the Exchange, but is purely a pretence, the brokers involved run the risk of detection and expulsion, which is to them a sentence of financial death.

There is, however, another class of transactions called "matched orders," which differ materially from those already mentioned, in that they are actual and enforceable contracts. We refer to that class of transactions engineered by some manipulator, who sends a number of orders simultaneously to different brokers, some to buy and some to sell. These brokers, without knowing that other brokers have countervailing orders from the same principal, execute their orders upon the floor of the Exchange, and the transactions become binding contracts; they cause an appearance of activity in a certain security which is unreal. Since they are legal and binding, we find a difficulty in suggesting a legislative remedy.

But where the activities of two or more brokers in certain securities become so extreme as to indicate manipulation rather than genuine transactions, the officers of the Exchange would be remiss unless they exercised their influence and authority upon such members in a way to cause them to desist from such suspicious and undesirable activity. As already stated, instances of continuous manipulation of particular securities are patent to every experienced observer, and could without difficulty be discouraged, if not prevented by prompt action on the part of the Exchange authorities.

Horace White (Chairman of the Hughes Commission) in "The Stock Exchange and the Money Market" (*Annals of the American Academy,* Nov., 1910):

The stock exchange is so large, its borrowings at times so colossal, that they affect the money supply of the world and are capable of absorbing the last dollar that can be tempted from the vaults of banks or the pockets of individuals in both hemispheres. This absorption may take place by the rise of prices of the securities traded in, or by the quantity offered, or both. Usually the demand for money is most imperative when the prices are highest and the quantities greatest.

The question whether this condition is an evil, is in effect the same as asking whether speculation is an evil. Upon this point Governor Hughes' committee on speculation in securities and commodities last year, reached the conclusion that to some persons it is an evil, and to others not, and that there is no way to prevent it, without putting an end to trading altogether. In that view the writer concurs. It should be added that speculation has a steadying effect on the market prices of both securities and commodities. To banish it would be to banish nine-tenths of the business, in which event the fluctuations in prices would be much greater, and the work of the manipulators more facile and dangerous, than now.

Mr. Muhleman, in the article from the *Independent* quoted above, says concerning manipulation:

When it is desired to "make a market" for a security, the practice is to create artificially a semblance of demand with the price going steadily upward; this leads the public to believe that there is an opportunity for profit. The mechanism employed is for the holders of a large majority (or all) of the shares to select one person as manager, being at all times prepared to buy any shares offered for sale by others at the market price. This, of course, requires a substantial sum of money to "carry" the shares, and this sum is borrowed from the banks on the pledge of the shares. The procedure has been properly called "manipulation," and in large part the plan is executed by what are known as "matched orders" and "washed sales." Thus, the manager simultaneously instructs one or more brokers to sell and other brokers to buy. At the outset he is the only buyer and the only seller, but gradually the activity of the stock attracts attention, and some outsider buys a few shares; then more join the movement. When all the shares to be "marketed" are disposed of the business is closed and profits are divided.

But it sometimes happens that before this time comes the outside holders or buyers want to sell, and the syndicate is compelled to take back the shares at the market price. Occasionally the price then falls violently and a panicky condition is developed, sometimes resulting in a crisis.

In almost every operation of the character it soon becomes known to the shrewd observers that a "manipulation" is on; the newspapers mention it and discuss it; brokers likewise refer to it. Yet the authorities of the Exchange have usually let it go on without check; if a crash came they have been loud in deploring the wickedness of the members engaged therein and have handed out punishments; if the scheme succeeded without catastrophe no need for action appeared, even if the inflated price of the shares fell violently. leaving the public to bear the losses. That is what the public that wants to engage in speculation is for.

In its nature the speculative business is such as to develop a marvelous acuteness of certain mental faculties in those members engaged in it. Some of them specialize along certain lines, and stimulated by an intense desire for gain or winning, the tendency is to accomplish the end in view by methods which strain the rules; occasionally rules are simply ignored. The risk of penalty, even to loss of membership, hangs over delinquent members. Yet many are apparently so accustomed to assumin risks that they take the chances. A study of the history of one of the severest failures in recent years disclosed that the firm had for quite a period indulged in almost every form of violation of trading principles with impunity.

The numerous amendments to the constitution bear witness how the governing board has been put to it to meet such instances in the past; it is, however, contended that they cannot devise rules to correct all vicious practices without impairing the usefulness of the system. Thus transactions engaged in merely for the purpose of artificial price making where every observer may be morally certain and some members absolutely know, that manipulation is in progress, are assumed to be beyond control because they are in form in accordance with the rules; it is regarded impossible to distinguish by rule between "matched orders" and bona fide ones, altho to the intelligent outsider matched orders look exactly like fictitious trades, which are prohibited. A continuance of this attitude will eventually force legislation that will make such distinction; for most manipulative price making clearly wrongs the public.

These questionable transactions are often deliberately carried on for the purpose of increasing the capital of the manipulators, borrowed from the banks on the securties. As a rule, banks loan up to 80 per cent. of the market price; it is obvious that whenever the market price of a security is advanced the amount of loans obtainable at the banks may be increased. Thus shares standing at 90 have a larger borrowing power than if valued at 60. In practice it seldom makes any difference how the price was made; but there are many notable instances where banks have taken cognizance of a reasonable belief that manipulation was going on, and have refused to advance the loaning power with the advance in price.

The Hughes Commission did not favor State regulation because it believed that the Exchange could regenerate itself, if it really wished to do so, and "make good" as to the avowed objects of its existence. But thru the influence of a majority of its members it persists in ignoring the need for regeneration; it insists that the transactions criticised are not vicious because they are thinly veiled by a formal contract; it places the transactions which the commission has practically characterized as gambling upon the same plane with such as are consistent with equitable principles of business. It assumes that since fictitious trades are forbidden they do not occur; a pleasing fiction which may some day be dissipated by the courts when the judges wake up to the gravity of the public wrong done thereunder.

Self-regulation would be so eminently preferable that legislation should be urged only as a last resort; but that such legislation will come if conditions continue much longer is quite certain. Perhaps the Congressional Committee will demonstrate the need therefor when it has completed its investigation.

———————

Sereno S. Platt, in "The Work of Wall Street" (1912); pp. 147 and 364.

No fictitious transactions are permitted on the floor under penalty of suspension for not more than one year. The common Street name for fictitious sales is "wash sales." When two brokers conspire together to make a pretended sale of a stock in order to give it a fictitous quotation, that is "a wash sale." It is practicable, however, for an outside operator, by using different brokers, some to sell and others to buy, by a process of "matched orders," as they are called, to give a fictitious value to a stock. This is, indeed, a common manipulative device, and has at times been carried to such extremes as to constitute very plain cases of fraud. While the brokers may be innocent tools of such a conspiracy, it has been argued that the Exchange might by some extension of its rules be able to reach the real conspirators, and in some way to prevent the evil. The Exchange aims at making every sale represent a genuine transaction.

Manipulation is of two kinds, these being well indicated by the Standard Dictionary definitions of the word: 1, adroit or skillful management; 2, fraudulent or deceptive management.

The latter is dishonest without qualification, and much of the odium which attaches to Wall Street is the result of this kind of stock manipulation, which, it may be said, is on the decline, due to restrictive and publicity methods. It consists mainly in the influencing of the course of prices by false reports. This is the only kind of manipulation that can be played by a small man. Any one can lie, and a lie has a wonderful power of communicating itself through the Street by a sort of wireless telegraphy. It is remarkable how many things one hears in the stockmarket that "aren't so." These false reports generally have a temporary effect on prices. But a lie persisted in is almost as good as the truth. A false report, therefore, may be so often repeated that in spite of official denials many will continue to believe in it, on the principle that where there is so much smoke there must be some fire. In such a case the effect on prices may be prolonged. The laws of the State make it a penal offense to originate or maliciously repeat falsehoods for the purpose of injuring the value of another's property, but it is difficult to track a lie to its lair.

In a suit brought against members of a syndicate charged with fraudulent manipulation, the complaint thus described its operations:

"Selling stocks to the public by improperly spread 'tips' and alleged information.

"Procuring loans from banking institutions throughout the country on stocks having fictitious values.

"Procuring the purchase of stock by means of alleged customers furnished to various stock brokerage houses throughout the country. The said customers would deposit on margin with the brokers a small proportion of the purchase price of the stocks, and these brokers would immediately buy for their supposed customers' account the stocks required, paying the syndicate's agents the full price thereof, these brokers advancing the difference from their own funds between such purchase price and the amount of margin deposited with them by their supposed customers."

In other words, by false tips and matched orders or wash sales the manipulators endeavored to establish fictitious quotations for their stocks. If, for instance, the security was actually worth only $50 a share, and by this means its market price was established at $120, the manipulators might be able either to sell to innocent investors at nearly 150 per cent. profit, or to obtain loans from country banks for amounts largely in excess of true value.

The late Bishop Potter, in an address at Yale, said truly: "The capitalist whom no honest man can hold converse with is he who artificially depresses values to the injury or loss of his fellow directors, or who withholds information regarding the condition of his company for his own personal advantage, or who by obscure bookkeeping deceives those whose money he holds in trust." He might also have added, "or who artificially advances prices to the injury," etc.

But there is a higher type of manipulation than this. It may be described as the fine art of buying and selling stocks to the best advantage. The high manipulator is the diplomatist of the Street. The diplomatist never lies, but he sometimes makes the worst appear the better reason. He does not lie, but he conceals his purposes so as not to disclose his operations.

Secrecy is, in fact, the first object of stock manipulation. It is quite impossible to tell in a few words how this is done. But it may be said briefly that the manipulator operates through several brokers at the same time. He may buy through some, and sell through others, so that no one, not even the brokers themselves, can be certain what his true position in the market is. Let us suppose that the manipulator represents a pool which has a large amount of stock to sell. It would not do to throw it upon the market at once, nor is it advisable that the Street should know that the pool is selling. So it may be buying with one hand and selling with the other, being careful, however, to sell more than it buys, and thus in the course of time the whole amount may be disposed of. There may have been a loss on, say 100,000 shares bought, but the profit on 150,000 shares sold may be so large as to make the entire operations very satisfactory to the members of the pool. In order to maintain the price of the stock it is trying to sell, the pool may find it necessary to buy other stocks, in order to give the general market the appearance of strength.

Capitalists controlling a railroad system sometimes consider it essential to "support" the stocks of the system, as the credit of the railroad, its ability to borrow money, and the ability of its individual directors to obtain the means for large operations depend, in no small measure, on the market value of its securities.

Likewise an underwriting syndicate which has undertaken to float a large issue of new securities is sometimes compelled to prepare the market to absorb them. This preparation may consist of an elaborate manipula-

tion of both money and stockmarkets, so as to make
rates for loans easy and prices of stocks attractive to
investors and speculators. As a preliminary to a bull
market it is often necessary first to clean out the weak
holders of stocks and depress prices to a point where
they look like bargains. The first act of a bull pool,
therefore, may actually be to bear prices. If the manipulator seeks to accumulate stocks, he will of course
try to break prices by a raid or attack on the market,
which is accomplished by furiously selling short. Suppose the manipulator discovers that long stock is held
in weak hands, and that there are many stop orders in
the market. He may institute a bear attack in order to
force liquidation, and uncover the stop orders, which,
as has already been explained, are orders to sell when
prices reach certain figures, generally marking the
limits of the customers' margins. The manipulator
may, and often does, strive to influence prices in New
York by having orders cabled from London, so as to
convey the impression that English investors are in the
market. This often has the desired effect on prices.

Charles A. Conant discusses manipulation in the *Atlan-
tic Monthly* (September, 1908):

The checking of undue manipulation is a highly
desirable object, but is not perhaps so important as
many persons imagine. Within certain limits, it might
even be contended that manipulation is justifiable. If
a financier or promoter has a new security which he
believes represents high value, he does not like to sit
with folded hands waiting for the public to discover
its value. To a certain extent the measures which he
may take to attract attention to the security are in the
nature of advertising. Large selling orders matched by

large buying orders, at a graded scale of ascending prices, bring the stock to public attention and make it talked about.

If this was the sole object of manipulation, and it was applied only to stocks whose real value needed only to be made known to attract purchasers, then even the rule of the stock exchange against matched orders would hardly need to be invoked for the protection of the public. But in fact, as every one knows, manipulation is often for the purpose of "unloading" securities of doubtful value and permitting the seller to pocket the proceeds of sales "at the top," and to buy back again at the price to which the stock descends after he has completed the process. Such manipulation is already contrary to the rules of the exchange but is difficult to prove. The broker who has a selling order is not usually the same as the one who has a buying order, and only rigid inquiry by a stock exchange committee, where manipulation was apparent or suspected, would ascertain the facts.

There is no doubt, however, that if the stock exchange should enpower its committee to take strong action in a few such cases, and the committee should assert its powers, a moral sentiment would be exercised against manipulation, which would be almost as complete as the influence which now obliges a broker or a client to acknowledge and execute contracts over the telephone, even though they result in heavy losses.

———

Henry C. Emery, in "Speculation in the United States" (1896); p. 176:

So far reference has been made only to the employment of honest methods in the attempts to turn the market. Other methods of a far different nature are not unknown. Among the most common of these is the spreading of false intelligence. In the desire to start the public buying or selling, false rumors of events affecting values may be circulated.

Such conditions are not unknown in the produce market, but the stock exchange affords an easier field for this and other evil practices. This is due to the fact that in the place of a half-dozen products of wide production and universal demand, the stock exchange presents a large number of securities of different kinds. The facts of crop supply, though they may be more accurately known by a few, are yet to some degree open to the scrutiny of all. But many of the numerous events that may change the value of a particular security can be known only to the insiders. Hence the temptation to spread false rumors is very great. The very sensitiveness of the market to every event which really affects values makes it equally sensitive to every rumor. Every possible occurrence is seized upon as an excuse to stimulate a new movement on the part of the public. Perhaps the evil is inseparable from the good, and in the main the stock exchange discriminates between false and true rumors more quickly and effectively than any other body. Nevertheless the power of such operators to deceive the public is productive of much harm.

Bradstreet's, writing of the stock market, says: "All of its votaries are not equally skilled in discovering the quality of any piece of news, or supposed news, nor are the rules of the game so stringent that the operator who can mislead his fellows or opponents without resorting to downright falsehood, is frowned upon with any severity. Something of the same kind might be said about every successful operator who ever graced Chapel Court, Wall Street, or the Frankfort or Paris Bourses. These examples, however, refer to the misuse of intelligence on a large scale—wholesale deception it might be termed." It may be added that the operator does not stop at "resorting to downright falsehood." The fact that the financial columns of some newspapers are purchasable for the insertion of such "news," blackens still more the nature of these operations.

Another method that may be resorted to is that of "wash sales," or "washed sales." If an operator wishes to make false prices on the floor, he may employ one broker to sell to another broker at prearranged prices. The price stands as a quotation, though the transaction is entirely fictitious. Such conduct, is needless to say, is economically and morally indefensible. Wash sales are forbidden by all the exchanges, but, except in flagrant cases, it is very difficult to detect them. In the case of a clique operating together, some members may sell to others and accomplish the same result. Similar practices occur without the collusion of brokers, that is, one set of brokers may be employed to sell and one to buy the same security in open market. The chances are that they will make their transactions together, in which case the operator has accomplished the same result as before. This is also a convenient method of giving a false appearance of activity to the trading in new securities in order to induce speculation or investment by the public. In such cases the conduct of the broker may be blameless, despite the tricky device in which he is made to take part.

There is one evil of stock speculation which is impossible in the case of produce. The value of wheat, or cotton, depends upon conditions which are entirely beyond the control of a few men. The value of a security, on the other hand, depends largely upon the policy of a group of directors. If they wish to speculate in the shares of their own companies they are in a position of extraordinary advantage. By means of one line of policy or another combined with the use of false information to the public, they may move the price to suit their private purposes. It may be that they will wreck the company in order to secure a permanent control of the property at a low price; or that they will destroy its credit in order to cover their own short sales; or that generally they will manipulate the price back and forth with a view to alternate profits.

Edwin R. A. Seligman (Professor of Political Economy in Columbia University), in "Principles of Economics" (1909); pp. 365 and 369:

Speculation is hence so perplexing a phenomenon because of its Janus-like aspect. So far as it has become the regular occupation of a class differentiated from other business men for this particular purpose, it subserves a useful and in modern times an indispensable function. The expert dealer on the exchanges, who studies and prejudges the market, will in the long run secure profits by reducing risks and steadying prices. In this wider sense speculative profits are earned like other profits.

On the other hand numbers of individuals without experience or ability are constantly taking "flyers" on the exchanges and gamble in securities or commodities as they would in cards. Speculation here is as demoralizing to earnest effort and thrift as is the lottery. Moreover even the professional dealer will often indulge in what we have termed sporadic speculation, and by an extensive manipulation of the market bring about the unsteadying of prices usually connected with a "squeeze" or a "corner." Difficult as it is to draw the line in practice, the distinction between the economic and uneconomic speculation is faintly recognized in the ordinary attitude toward the bucket-shop as compared to the Stock Exchange.

It will be more clearly appreciated in the future when the exchanges themselves exercise a more rigid scrutiny over the actions of their members, and when business ethics will be lifted to a higher plane of social responsibility. At present speculation has its economic abuses as well as its economic function.

The recent anti-option laws of Germany have either been ineffectual or have done harm in preventing the legitimate and economic benefits of speculation. To prohibit speculation is to prevent the good as well as the evil. Taxation, again, is applicable only to certain aleatory profits. The effort to tax speculative profits encounters the well-nigh insuperable difficulty of causing the tax to be actually borne by the recipient of the profits. Finally, the prohibition of speculative prices is virtually equivalent to the futile prohibition of speculation itself.

The British Parliamentary Commission (1878) reported as to "extravagant speculation":

We do not think it is practical to make bargains entered into for the purpose of speculation or gambling any more illegal than they are at present, and we do not purpose any change in the law.

At the same time we are satisfied from the evidence that gambling to an enormous extent does exist at the present day, in securities of all kinds, and that it is carried on both on the Stock Exchange and by persons outside of it who are not members of the Stock Exchange. The proceedings of the Bankruptcy Court are constantly bringing to light excesses of this kind, committed by persons who, having lost money in trade, seek to re-establish themselves by desperate ventures in speculation. Evil practices also of the same kind are rife among persons of very limited means, who are not in such circumstances as to justify a broker in speculating for them.

It is to some extent a matter of surprise that brokers should be found willing to undertake such business, seeing that by the rules of the Stock Exchange the broker becomes personally responsible to any other member of the house with whom he deals for the fulfilment of the contract which he makes on his principal's behalf. But we have been told that much of this gambling business, so far as it is transacted by members of the house, is done by the younger and more necessitous members, who, having little substantial business, are driven to accept business of this kind with its attendant risks.

We have sought without success for a means of preventing such practices but something we think, may be done to restrain them to some extent. Although it be true that when a client orders a broker to buy stock for him the broker may not in some cases know whether his client intends to purchase as an investment or speculation, it is equally true that after a few transactions the broker will become aware, both from the amounts of stock bought and sold, and the way such bargains are dealt with on the settling day, of the nature of the business in which his client is engaged.

The committee of the Stock Exchange might, therefore, very well hold a restraining hand over any of their own members who should turn out to have lent themselves to extravagant speculation or to any speculation by those who had no adequate means. The committee should, we think, in cases where bankruptcy or insolvency has resulted from practices of this kind, call the broker through whose agency the insolvency was brought about, to account, visiting him with severe punishment in the absence of reasonable exculpation.

We are of the opinion that the existing system may with advantage be modified, remarking that the changes which we recommend are such as can be carried out by the Stock Exchange themselves without the assistance or interference of the Legislature.

III. On Short Sales and Manipulation.

Samuel H. Ordway, who was a member of the Hughes Commission, discusses manipulation and short selling in *Scribners Magazine* (Sept. 1909):

> It is extremely difficult, if not impossible, to devise any safe system of legislation to restrict the manipulation of prices. No one has yet been able to suggest a form of statute which will prevent improper manipulation of prices and will at the same time permit legitimate transactions on a large scale.

> Short selling has been the subject of constant attention and very serious criticism from the public and the press. It is difficult to see why it is economically or morally wrong to agree to sell something that one does not possess but expects to obtain in the future, any more than it is to agree to buy what one has not the money to pay for at the present time but expects to have the money to pay for later on.

> Contracts and agreements to sell and deliver in the future commodities which one does not possess at the time of the contract is comon in all forms of business. The manufacturer sells what he has not yet produced; he must do so to keep his factory open and his

hands employed the year around; the farmer agrees to sell his growing crop; the contractor agrees to deliver the house built of bricks he has not yet purchased and with labor he has not yet contracted for; and so on *ad infinitum.*

While undoubtedly the short selling of securities may temporarily cause a serious lowering of prices and even a panic, still in the long run it tends to steady prices and to prevent both rising and falling markets from going to extremes. It must be remembered that the man who has sold short must some day buy back in order to return the stock he has borrowed to make the short sale.

If short sales were prevented, or even substantially limited, it would be possible for daring manipulators to run prices up to an abnormal height, from which they would come down with a crash that would ruin all involved, as in the case of the South Sea bubble and John Law's Mississippi Scheme. Short sales made by speculators whose judgment enable them accurately to forecast the future, increasing as prices mount upward, always tend to prevent extremes from being reached.

———

F. W. Taussig (Professor of Economics in Harvard University), in "Principles of Economics" (1912), p. 166:

Unmistakable as are the evils of speculative gambling, it is exceedingly difficult to check them by legislation, still more to put an end to them. The common law already makes void transactions which are sales in form merely, and which contemplate a settlement only of the difference between present and future price. But on the exchanges all transactions purport to be, and in strict legal effect are, for the actual delivery of the commodities.

An obvious remedial measure is to prohibit buying and selling for future delivery, since it is in connection with such contracts that the gambling operations most often take place. But this would put an end, also, to the benefits which the community gets from contracts for futures; and it is a question whether the loss would not outweigh the gain. The common opinion of American and English economists is against the prohibition of future contracts, which, so far as grain is concerned, has been put into effect in Germany. Yet the evils of speculative gambling are so great that something may be risked for the purpose of lessening them. Lotteries and avowed gambling houses have been prohibited, and the law does its utmost to prevent wholesale betting on horse races; and all it can do to stamp out other forms of gambling is welcome.

No doubt, the most effective remedy would be a better moral standard for all industry, and an aroused public opinion against all kinds of gambling. But the worship of wealth, and the well-nigh universal desire to make money on easy terms, even though at the expense of others, together with the close association of this sort of speculation with business dealing rightly deemed legitimate, render it difficult to bring public opinion to bear.

In stock exchange speculation the problems appear in accentuated form. Here, too, advantages are to be set against evils. The advantages, it is true, are of a different sort from those secured by grain and cotton exchanges. They arise, not from the lessening of fluctuations or the facilitation of large-scale dealings, but from the promotion of investment. They are real and important. But the evils are no less real, and are intensified by the unusual ease entering on the transactions.

Stock exchange securities are ideally homogenous and standardized. One share of a given corporation's stock is precisely as good as any other share. If it is easy for anyone to buy grain or cotton, even though he has never looked at the articles, it is still easier for any one to buy stocks and bonds, even though he knows nothing about the corporation that issues them. At the same time, fluctuations in the prices of securities are large and frequent. Opinions regarding their probable course depends (or seems to depend) quite as much on general judgment and general prospects as on expert information. Hence rampant speculation, by outsiders and insiders.

The professional speculators and dealers get the advantage of the miscellaneous public, both because they are better informed regarding the real prospects of the enterprises whose securities are dealt in, and because they are (by a process of quasi-natural selection) persons shrewd in judging human nature and quick to take advantage of the irresolute. Yet notwithstanding the constant losses, there is an unfailing stream of persons who take fliers on the stock exchange. There are probably few Americans of the well-to-do classes who have not at one time or another tried their hands at a stock speculation; and there are a great many who habitually gamble in stocks. The immense majority of these dealings are concentrated at the New York Stock Exchange, which is at once the greatest institution in the world for facilitating investment and the greatest of gambling hells.

The evil from the situation arises not only or chiefly from the losses of the unsuccessful speculators. What these lose, others gain, and usually there is not much to choose between winners and losers. The economic loss arises primarily from the waste of much brains and energy on unproductive doings. The waste is more than that of the labor given directly—the labor of the brokers and their understrappers, and of the speculators themselves. It is increased by the demoralization of many men in the community who take no great direct share in speculation. Like all gambling, it distracts from the sober, continuous work on which the common welfare rests. Morally, it is no less harmful. In every aspect the evil is one of the greatest in contemporary society.

It must be frankly confessed that no really promising remedies have been suggested. Some excrescenses have been aimed at in recent proposals for reform in New York—proposals which look to improvement through the revision and enforcement of the rules made by the exchanges for themselves. Such things as rigging of the market, "wash sales," manipulation of prices with intent to deceive, are to be thus prevented. But even if all of these tricks were cut out, the main evil would remain.

In Germany a more drastic remedy has been tried,— the requirement of publicity in stock dealings, through enrollment of names and transactions on a register open to general inspection. It is expected that men will refrain from stock gambling, as they will from many doings of doubtful aspect, if they must be seen in the act. Such a requirement would be met in the United States by the objection that it intrudes on the sacrosanct secrecy of business, an objection commonly brought against public supervision of every sort, yet in itself of little weight.

Much more serious is the objection that in Germany the regulation has in fact had little effect; stock speculation has remained much the same in character and amount. Possibly this is because of the difficulty of effective enforcement. At all events, though the evil is there, no clear remedy of a direct sort is in sight.

Greater regularity of all industry would lessen fluctuation in values, and so lessen speculation; but this would be at the cost of 'progress. Better public opinion would lessen "outside" speculation; but the enlightenment of public opinion proceeds very slowly.

Arthur Twining Hadley (President of Yale University), in "Economics" (1911); pp. 106-112:

Unfortunately there is a mass of speculation which is not legitimate—which is either pure gambling or something worse. If a man goes into the purchase of grain or cotton, not because he foresees that it will be wanted, but for the excitement of the wager, he is doing the same kind of business as the man who bets on a horse race or on cards. The amount of these gambling transactions veiled under the forms of commerce has become very large. In many cases, it has assumed the proportions of a public evil.

The sales of certain commercial staples, such as wheat, cotton or petroleum, in the New York market are in some years fifty times as great as the actual deliveries. Of the transactions in stocks, perhaps an equally small proportion represent purchases for investment. A large part of such sales and purchases are made on margins; the buyer not paying or intending to pay the full amount, but depositing with his broker a sufficient sum to secure the latter from loss, and receiving or paying at the completion of the transaction an amount corresponding to the change in price of the commodity purchased. The narrower the margin, the greater is the chance of gain or loss in proportion to the capital invested, and the higher are the stakes to the gambler on either side.

Here, as elsewhere, high stakes constitute a temptation to unfair play. If the outside public, as frequently happens, has bought securities or produce in ill-grounded hope of a rise in price, the professional operators will speculate for a fall and try to insure its advent by spreading false reports of every kind. If, on the other hand, a large number of operators have made contracts to deliver securities or produce which they do not possess, a few men with large capital will often try to lock up the whole available supply of such commodities, and compel those who have made the contracts to purchase the means of filling them at an exorbitant figure. Such an operation is known as a corner; and its success is made possible by the number of speculative contracts which must be filled within a limited period of time.

The man who thus attempts to manipulate the market, lowering prices by false reports or raising them by factitious scarcity, is doing the same kind of business as a man who "pulls" horses or stacks cards. In fact, he is doing worse; for the men who suffer from false running or from card sharping are those who voluntarily go into the business of betting; while the knavish speculator may hurt to some degree not only speculators, but also producers and consumers—the producers by the deceit, the consumers by his combinations to raise prices. The direct harm done to producers and consumers by these means is very likely much less than is generally supposed; in the first place, because successful corners are relatively few, and, in the second place, because the profits of one group of speculators are for the most part made at the expense of other groups. But the indirect harm to business methods and business morals is incalculable.

So great has been the extent of this evil that many have desired to see an entire prohibition of contracts for future delivery of things which a man does not possess at the time; but this is obviously out of the question. It would prevent operations like those of the cotton broker or the lumber merchant, which economize the capital if the comunity and have become a necessary feature in modern business life. It would be attended by great and disastrous irregularity in prices. Any legislation of this kind, in order to be successful, must be so contrived as to affect the gambling transactions and leave the legitimate ones comparatively untouched.

It is extremely difficult to make this distinction by law. It cannot be based on the subject-matter of the transaction. The illegitimate speculations deal with the same articles as the legitimate ones. Sometimes when public indignation has been aroused by the operation of brokers in certain lines there have been attempts made to stop all transactions in those lines; but they have usually proved disastrous.

Nor can the distinction be based on the form of the transaction. In England the law attempts to enforce a requirement of actual delivery. But in the majority of speculative commodities delivery is made, not by turning over the product itself, but by a warehouse receipt. The physical delivery of a thousand bales of cotton every time the right to that cotton changed hands would involve an absurd waste of power. A warrant is all which can be delivered. But a warrant for delivery can be passed as many times as the exigencies of the law require. Instances are on record where such warrants have changed hands fifty times before reaching the actual consumer. The spirit of the law requiring delivery can thus be evaded. It is almost as easy to evade laws which prohibit the settlement of transactions by the payment of margins—transactions where there is no delivery of goods, but a payment of money from one party to the other, based on a change in value of the goods. Where it can be proved that this was the original intent of the transaction it is easy to stamp it as gambling; but a very slight change in form is sufficient to enable such operations to be continued under a nominal compliance with the letter of the law and in open opposition to its spirit.

The difference between legitimate speculation and gambling lies neither in the subject-matter nor in the form of the transaction, but in its intent and purpose. Legitimate speculation involves anticipation of the needs of the market and a power to assume risks in making contracts to meet these deeds. A failure to fulfill either of these requirements makes the operation an undesirable one for the public to tolerate. If a man, instead of anticipating the needs of the market, attempts to manipulate that market by combinations and corners, any gain that he makes is usually at the expense of the public.

A stricter enforcement of laws with regard to conspiracy, and, what is more to the purpose, a better understanding by the business community of the distinction between what is good and bad public policy in this matter, would do a great deal to remedy some of the worst evils with which speculation is attended.

Henry Rogers Seager (Professor of Political Economy in Columbia University), in "Introduction to Economics" (1905); p. 175.

Some of the shrewdest and best-informed men in the United States find it profitable to devote much of their time to studying the conditions of supply and demand with reference to each of the great staple products. They make mistakes in their calculations of course,

and very often buy or sell for future delivery at prices
widely different from those which actually prevail when
the future time arrives. But they are less apt to make
mistakes than men who are without their special talent
and training, and on the whole their operations have a
decidedly steadying influence on the prices of the commodities in which they deal. Even more important is
the service they render in assuming risks in regard to
price changes which otherwise all enterpreneurs would
have to share and in making it possible for conservative
producers to know just what prices they will have to
pay for needed materials months before they have
occasion to use them.

Not a little criticism has been directed against dealings in futures on the ground that such transactions
are highly speculative. This cannot be denied, but it
must be remembered that it is not merely the dealings
in futures, but the future itself, that is uncertain. If
such dealings can be confined to the men most competent to make accurate predictions, their tendency
will clearly be to lessen the uncertainties of business.
The operation of such men prepare the whole business
community for changes that are inevitable, long before
less observing people see any reason for them.

Unfortunately the question of the social expediency
of dealings in futures is mixed up with the wider question of the expediency of stock and commodity speculation as it is now carried on in the financial centres
of the country. It is notorius that this speculation is
not confined to men who make it a business and are
trained for it in the hard school of experience, but that
it is indulged in intermittently by a great army of
men and women whose only qualifications are a taste
for gambling and the consciousness of having money
to invest. To the extent that these uninformed speculators accept the leadership of men of sound judg-

ment and wide experience, their presence simply increases the influence which such men can bring to bear when they deem imminent a change in prices. Too often, however, the mob follows after some false prophet and make him more of a power for evil than he could be if he had only his own wealth to misdirect, or is deceived by some sagacious but unscrupulous operator who circulates false reports designed to cheapen what he wants to buy or to enhance in price the things he wants to sell. In either case its influence is altogather pernicious. How to confine speculation to those who have aptitude and training for it and to discourage stock and commodity gambling is one of the economic problems of the day.

Charles A. Conant, in "Wall Street and the Country" (1904) ; pp. 88 and 111.

The wrongs which have been perpetrated on the exchanges have come largely from perversion of their essential functions as the public mirror of values. It has been the dream of great manipulators to warp this mirror so that it would mislead the public to their own profit. The success which such manipulations have attained has, however, been greatly exaggerated in the public mind. It is truthfully declared by Courtois, in his Traité des Opérations de Bourse et de Change, that a fictitious movement, even on the part of the most powerful operators, cannot overcome the natural tendencies of values, and that the most that can be accomplished is to sometimes hasten or retard slightly the certain effect of a foreseen event.

Some of those who admit the value of the stock market have subjected to severe criticism those who speculate for the fall of stocks. One reads constantly of the "bears" trying to acomplish such and such results by depressing securities. Napoleon had a long talk with Mollien, his Minister of Finance, in seeking to demonstrate that those who sold "short," in the belief that national securities would fall, were traitors to their country. He argued that if these men were selling national securities for furture delivery at less than their present value, they were guilty of treason to the State. But Mollien replied in substance: "These men are not the ones who determine the price; they are only expressing their judgment upon what it will be. If they are wrong; if the credit of our State is to be maintained in the future at its former high standard, in spite of your military preparations, these men will suffer the penalty by having to make delivery at the price for which they sold, for they must go into the market and buy at the price then prevailing. It is their judgment not their wish, that they express."

The short seller—the "bear" of the money market—is often one of its greatest benefactors. He calls a halt on reckless speculation, and his acts, tending to depress prices, produce their natural result of repressing extravagant inflation of values, if his judgment is sustained by facts and by the judgment of other men. If it is simply a mistaken individual judgment, he pays for his error in cash to some one with a more hopeful and saner judgment.

Irving Fisher (Professor of Political Economy in Yale University), in "The Nature of Capital and Income" (1906), pp. 295 and 300:

Where risks cannot be reduced to a statistical basis, and therefore cannot be insured against, recourse is often had to the shifting of the risk into the hands of those who are willing to take it. Such persons are speculators. A speculator is usually one in whom the caution factor is not so pronounced as in the ordinary individual. In extreme cases he tends to become a simple gambler. The distinction between a speculator and a gambler, however, is usually fairly well marked. A gambler seeks and makes risks which is not necessary to assume, whereas the speculator is one who merely volunteers to assume those risks of business which must inevitably fall somewhere. A speculator is also usually fitted for his work by special knowledge, so that the risk to him, owing to superior foresight, is at the outset less than it would be to others.

The indiscriminate prejudice against all speculation, which is so often met with, beside the point; for, were there no speculators, the same risks would have to be borne by those less fitted to bear them. The chief evils of speculation flow from the participation of the general public who lack the special knowledge, and enter the market in a purely gambling spirit. In addition to suffering the usual evil consequences of gambling, they produce evil consequences for the non-partcipating public by causing fictitious fluctuations in the values of the products or property in which they speculate.

The evils of speculation are particularly acute when as generally happens with the investing public, the forecasts are not made independently. Were it true that each individual speculator made up his mind independently of every other as to the future course of events, the errors of some would probably be offset by those of others. But as a matter of fact, the mistakes of the common herd are usually in the same direction. Like sheep, they all follow a single leader. How easily they are led is shown by the effect on the

stock market in the year 1904, when Thomas Lawson
published scarehead advertisements in the newspapers
advising the public to sell certain securities.

Short selling, binding the future to the past, enables
the specialist to guarantee to the general public a
definite foreseen series of events. The beneficial effect
to the public, in saving useless stocks and reserves,
in producing more intelligent direction of enterprises,
and in encouraging accumulation through greater certainty of its future benefits, is both obvious and great.
Risk is one of the direct economic evils, and all of the
devices which aid in overcoming it—whether increased
guaranties, safeguards, foresight, insurance, or legitimate speculation—represent a great boon to humanity.

LEGISLATION ON SHORT SALES.

I. England.

The popular outcry that arose in England after the bursting of the South Sea bubble resulted, in 1734, in the passage of Sir John Barnard's "Act to Prevent the Infamous Practice of Stock-Jobbing." The preamble recited:

> Whereas, great inconveniences have arisen, and do daily arise, by the wicked, pernicious, and destructive practice of stock-jobbing, whereby many of His Majesty's good subjects have been and are diverted from pursuing and exercising their lawful trades and vocations to the utter ruin of themselves and their families, to the great discouragement of industry, and to the manifest detriment of trade and commerce.

The act forbade bargains for "puts or refusals"; also "the evil practice of compounding or making up differences"; and furthermore prohibited all sales of stock by parties not owning the same, under penalty of £100 for each transaction. The object aimed at by Sir John Barnard's statute was only partially attained, for the courts held that the statute did not apply to foreign stocks nor to shares in companies, but only to English public stocks. The law was a dead letter. It was only resorted to occasionally by welching speculators. In 1860 it was repealed, the repeal act reciting that Sir John Barnard's Act "imposed unnecessary restrictions on the making of contracts for sale and transfer of public stocks and securities."

Leeman's Act of 1867 declared all sales of Bank stock, without a specification of the share numbers in the contract, void. This was an attempt to prevent the short selling of Bank stock. This has also proved a dead letter England, to-day, has no law on the statute books restricting speculation.

After six centuries of legislation against speculation, England finally removed all restrictions on speculation. But, in 1877, in response to popular attacks on speculation, a Royal Commission was appointed "to inquire into the origin, objects, present constitution, customs and usages of the London Stock Exchange." The report of this commission, with the evidence, was published in a Parliamentary Blue Book (1878). The Commissioners' report is of interest in this country chiefly because:

1. It absolutely upheld the purpose of the Stock Exchange and the legitimacy of speculation in securities.

2. It pointed out the dangers of attempting to force external control on the Exchange.

II. France.

Short sales on the Paris Bourse were specifically legalized by the law of 1885. In the publications of the National Monetary Commission (1911) the history of this legislation is told in detail by E. Vidal in his monograph on "The History and Methods of the Paris Bourse." Extracts from his discussion follow:

A law of March 28, 1885, recognized as legal all transactions for future delivery (marches à terme) even those which are settled by paying the difference—

and removed those special obligations imposed upon
stockbrokers which were of a nature rendering such
operations impossible.

The law on time-bargains (marches á terme) is
very important from an economic standpoint. Not
only does it indicate a social progress, in that it removed the monstrous immorality which was formerly
widespread and which consisted in permitting speculators to decline to pay their differences by presenting
the plea of gambling, but it indicates, besides, a philo-
sophical progress—a progress in the general trend of
thought. The time-bargain is not simply a contract
the settlement of which is postponed to a certain date,
one which works itself out in time and space; it is
a contract upon generalized merchandise.

For a long time financiers, economists and business
men clamored for legal recognition of dealings for
future delivery, and even speculative bargains, "short"
or "long" sales of stock (operations á decouvert), or
of such that close by paying the difference.

As early as in 1801 Count Mollien, while talking
with the First Consul, told him: "It is true, General,
that these transactions (marches á terme) were pro-
scribed before the Revolution by a council's decision;
but when it is seen that they have never been more
numerous than since that time, we might ask ourselves
whether it is the law or the dealings for future delivery
(marches á terme) which are to be found fault with.
When we then consider the course of all civil transactions, we see everything resolved into transactions
for future delivery; through them towns are supplied,
armies are maintained; on them are based all great
commercial combinations; we praise the cleverness
of the merchant who purchases provisions for a sum
tenfold his capital, because he has so well gauged the

requirements of consumption that the sale of his goods is assured him before reaching the maturity fixed for the payment.

"Why should not that principle, which is held in esteem in all European centers, be recognized in that place called the Bourse? Will anyone object that on the Bourse transactions for future delivery are not always bona fide? Should we then give up bills of exchange because dishonest merchants make ill use of them?

"If abuses have been introduced into Bourse transactions, the blame should be laid on the administration of justice, which places these transactions beyond the reach of the law; if they break public faith, the less should the courts refuse to take cognizance of the fact. Their duty is to search for and punish that breach.

"When a free man has involved himself in reckless engagements, it is their fulfillment that he must find the penalty for his folly and his bad faith; the efficacy of the penalty is to be found in the warning it leaves; and, surely, to declare the object of the offense void for the benefit of the more guilty person, was not a salutary warning given by the jurisprudence of 1786?

"Bourse transactions have a peculiar character, in that the two contracting parties, unknown to one another, bind themselves, through the mediation of a stock broker, who is the representative of the low (l'homme de la loi) ; he is responsible before the law for all his actions; therefore the low should not decline to pass upon any of these actions.

"The common objections to Bourse contracts are: One cannot sell that which one does not own, and the law cannot recognize a bargain which should never

have been made. In the main, these objections are
merely begging the question; it seems to me that the
law should not protect that which it cannot punish;
it should not prohibit in Paris a mode of dealing sanc-
tioned through long practice in London and Amsterdam.

"I do not claim that time-bargains (marches à
terme) are free from abuses, but I demand that, in
order to repress these abuses, the contracting parties
be judged according to common law on contracts."

The transactions for the account of the Bourse were,
nevertheless, if not prohibited, at least made impractic-
able, through the texts of the old ordinances on the
Bourse—the Council decisions of 1774, 1785 and 1788.
The decree of 27 Prairial, year X., exacted that the
stockbroker should have on hand the securities to be
disposed of and the funds necessary for purchases.
No doubt, to meet the requirements of the times,
transactions for the account were considered as allow-
able, provided they were made in good earnest. At
any rate, if they were not made good by depositing the
securities or the cash, they were illegal.

In 1867, the Imperial Government appointed a
commission to inquire into the question of time-bargains. M. L. Chevallier, a member of the commission
of 1867, made a remarkable report on the subject,
concluding in favor of the necessity that the law recognize dealings for future delivery.

On February 8, 1882, the Paris Chamber of Commerce passed a resolution calling on the Government
for a modification of the existing laws, M. Gustave
Roy preparing the report.

In the Chamber of Deputies two members, M. M.
Alfred Naquet and Lagrange, introduced a joint proposition tending to recognize dealings on the "long" and
"short" accounts (operations a decouvert) as legal.

The Government, on its part, appointed a special commission to study the question.

The law on dealings for future delivery (marches à terme) was promulgated on April 8, 1885. Having been finally voted upon on March 28, it is generally known as the law of March 28, 1885. Dealings for future delivery are recognized as legal. They were legal before; on that point the law aimed only to do away with the surrounding uncertainties which resulted from the special regulations made for stockholders. Thus, in the terms of that law, no one can, in regard to operations for future delivery, please article 1965 of the Code Civil, according to which the law grants no recourse to a party for the payment of a gambling debt. Article 1965 of the Code Civil is not repealed, but it cannot be applied to transactions closing by a difference.

III. Germany.

The costly experience of the German people in attempting to kill speculation is discussed by Henry Crosby Emery in a paper, "Ten Years Regulation of the Stock Exchange in Germany," in the *Yale Review* (May, 1909). Professor Emery thus summarizes the results of the operation of the German Bourse Law:

(1) Fluctuations in prices have been increased rather than deminished. The corrective influence of the bear side of the market having been restricted, the tendency to an inflated bull movement was increased in times of prosperity. This in turn made the danger of radical collapse all the greater in proportion as the bull movement was abnormal. The greater funds needed to carry stocks on a cash basis further increased the danger when collapse was threatened

The result was an increased incentive to reckless speculation and manipulation. Says German Government's report of 1907: "The dangers of speculation have been increased, the power of the market to resist one-sided movements has been weakened, and the possibilities of misusing inside information have been enlarged."

(2) The money market has been increasingly demoralized through the greater fluctuations in demand for funds to carry speculative cash accounts. The New York method is held in abhorrence by German financiers, who attribute to it, in large part, the wild fluctuations in New York call rates, the 'frequent "money panics" and the tendency to reckless "jobbery." In proportion as the new Berlin methods approached the cash delivery system of New York, these evils have appeared there.

(3) The business of the great banks has been increased at the expense of their smaller rivals. The prohibition of trading for the account made it difficult for the latter to carry out customer's orders because the new methods required large supplies of both cash and securities. Furthermore, an increasing share of the business of the large banks came to be settled by offsets among their customers, and the actual exchange transactions became a proportionally small part of the total transfers.

(4) This had a twofold effect. Business within the banks is done on the basis of exchange prices, but these became more fluctuating and subject to manipulation as the quantity of exchange dealings were diminished and were concentrated in a few hands. The advantages of a broad open market were lost. The object of the act had been to lessen the speculative influence over industrial undertakings. Its effect was to increase it.

(5) Finally the effect of interference increased cost, and legal uncertainty was to drive business to foreign exchanges and diminish the power of the Berlin Exchange in the field of international finance. The number of agencies of foreign houses increased four or fivefold and much German capital flowed into other centers, especially London, for investment or speculation. This in turn weakened the power of the Berlin money market, so that even the Reichs-bank has at times felt its serious effects.

Samuel H. Ordway, reviewing the effects of the German attempt at regulation, in *Scribner's Magazine* (Sept. 1909), says:

This German Bourse Law of 1896 attempted to do the very things which have been so generally advocated of late in this country, that is, to prevent manipulation, to restrict short sales and to prevent what is known at stock-gambling by the uninformed public.

It was a disastrous failure. Legitimate business was largely driven out of the country, and was transacted upon the London and Paris exchanges through remissiers, who acted as local agents for foreign brokers. With very few exceptions, persons speculating in securities and commodities refused to register, and such transactions as took place in Germany were subject to the risk of repudiation. In some cases speculators dealt on both sides of the market, that is, bought and sold the same security at the same time; if the security went up, they endeavored to carry out the transactions in which they had bought and repudiated the other; if it went down, they insisted upon their sale and repudiated their purchase. Even where honest dealers intended to carry out their transactions, it often happened that, in case of their death, their executors were compelled to treat the transactions as illegal. At a result, such business as was done in Germany fell largely into the hands of the large banks.

The injury to German business and to Germany's financial prestige was so enormous that public opinion gradually changed, and in course of time came to demand the repeal or amendment of the law, and 1908 the law was very materially amended so as practically to do away with the system requiring the registration of speculators and to permit short sales of securities within certain limitations. The experience of Germany is valuable and instructive, and shows the danger of injury to legitimate and necessary business resulting from extreme efforts by the State to control and eliminate the evils connected with speculation.

IV. United States.

The only attempt ever made by the American government to restrict speculation was the Gold Speculation Act of 1864. This was repealed fifteen days later because the restriction of speculation in gold intensely aggravated the evils that the public thought were due to the speculation. President Hadley, in his "Economics," relates what happened at that time:

In the year 1864 the large issue of paper currency had driven gold out of circulation and caused it to be bought and sold as a commodity. Much of it was in the hands of speculators. When its price rose more than 100 per cent. it was supposed by the public that a part of this increase was due to the operations of these speculators. All gold speculation was therefore forbidden by statute. Under the excitement of public opinion in time of war this statute was enforced to a far greater degree than could have been done in peace. The effect was precisely the opposite of what had been anticipated. Every man who was engaged in foreign trade had to provide security for being able to make gold payments in the immediate future, if called upon to do so. Being prevented from dealing with speculators, he now had to accumulate a reserve of his own. This caused an increased demand for gold at a time when it was unusually difficult to maintain an adequate supply. Under two weeks operation of the act the price of a hundred gold dollars rose from about two hundred paper dollars to very nearly three hundred. So obvious was its evil effect that it was hurriedly repealed as a means of preventing further commercial disasters.

The heavy speculation in paper money and in bank shares in the period of financial distress at the outbreak of the second war with England led to the passage by the New York State Legislature, in 1812, of the only anti-speculation act ever on the New York Statute books. This was "An Act to Regulate Sales at Public Auction and to Prevent Stock Jobbing." It provided:

That all contracts, written or verbal, hereafter to be made, for the sale or transfer, and all wagers concerning the prices present or future, or any certificate or evidence of debt due by or from the United States or any separate State, or any share or shares of stock of any bank, or any share or shares of stock of any company established, or to be established, by any law of the United States, or any individual State, shall be, and such contracts are hereby declared to be absolutely void; and both parties are hereby discharged from the lien and obligation of such contract or wager; unless the party contracting to sell and transfer the same shall at the time of making such contract be in the actual possession of the certificate or other evidence of such debt or debts, share or shares, or to be otherwise entitled in his own right or duly authorized or empowered by some person so entitled to transfer said certificate, evidence, debt, or debts, share or shares so to be contracted for. And the party or parties who may have paid any premium, differences or sums of money in pursuance of any contract, hereby declared to be void, shall and may recover all such sums of money, together with damages and costs, by action on the case, in assumpsit for money had and received for the use of the plaintiff to be brought in any court of record.

This law was aimed at short-selling, but as it merely provided a means by which a speculator might welch on a contract, and did not forbid short-selling, it served no purpose. The act of 1812 was a dead letter. In 1858, it was repealed, and short-selling was declared to be legal. The act of 1858 reads:

No contract, written or verbal, hereafter made for the purchase, sale, transfer or delivery of any certificate or other evidence of debt due by or from the United States, or any separate State, or if any share or interest in the stock of any bank, or of any company incorporated under the laws of the United States, or of any individual State, shall be void or voidable for want of consideration, or because of the non-payment of any consideration, or because the vendor, at the time of making such contract, is not the owner or possessor of the certificate or certificates, or other evidence of such debt, share or interest.

The laws of the various States of the Union affecting speculation are a hodge-podge. A few of the States have statutes similar to the New York statute legalizing short sales of commodities and securities. These States are Wisconsin, Louisiana, California, Montana, North Dakota and South Dakota. Nearly all the Cotton States now have laws against cotton futures. Other States have laws against futures, short sales, corners, forestalling and speculation in general.

In Board of Trade of the City of Chicago *v.* Christie Grain & Stock Company, 198 U. S., 247, the Supreme Court, speaking by Mr. Justice Holmes, said:

The plaintiff's chamber of commerce is, in the first place, a great market, where, through its eighteen hundred members, is transacted a large part of the grain and provision business of the world. Of course, in a modern market contracts are not confined to sales for immediate delivery. People will endeavor to forecast the future and to make agreements according to their prophecy. Speculation of this kind by competent men is the self-adjustment of society to the probable. Its value is well known as a means of avoiding or mitigating catastrophes, equalizing prices and providing for periods of want. It is true that the success of the strong induces imitation by the weak, and that incompetent persons bring themselves to ruin by undertaking to speculate in their turn.

But legislatures and courts generally have recognized that the natural evolutions of a complex society are to be touched only with very cautious hands and that such coarse attempts at a remedy for the waste incident to every social function as a simple prohibition and laws to stop its being are harmful and vain.

This court has upheld sales of stock for future delivery and the substitution of parties provided for by the rules of the Chicago Stock Exchange. Clews *v.* Jamieson, 182 U. S., 461.

Judge Barnard, in the Circuit Court of the District of Columbia, in a Stock Exchange case, said:

A short sale is not a gambling operation. The law defines a gambling operation to be one where the parties make a contract of purchase and sale without intent on the part of either to deliver or receive the article which is the subject of the contract. Nothing passes betwen the parties beyond the money from loser to winner, and nothing else was intended to pass. This is a mere bet—a gamble. But where actual delivery is made of the goods contracted to be sold and received the transaction becomes a commercial one. The testimony shows that in a short sale delivery of the stocks sold is made and the purchase price is paid. That fact establishes it as a commercial transaction. It may be speculative; it is speculative; but commercial transactions generally are more or less speculative, the speculative element in them varying mainly in degree.

LEGISLATION ON MANIPULA-
TION.

Dishonest manipulation of the speculative markets is a crime under the common law.

John R. Dos Passos, in "Stock Brokers and Stock Exchanges" (1905), discusses this subject in detail. The following excerpts are of interest:

The modern rule seems to be this; that the offences of "regrating," "forestalling" and "engrossing," as they were defined under the statutes of Edward, no longer exist (unless revived by express legislation) either in England or in this country, so far as individual action or property is concerned; but in place thereof the common law declares that combinations or conspiracies by several persons to engross or absorb any particular necessary staple of life to the detriment of the public, are illegal, and the subject of indictment.

The case of Rex *vs.* Waddington illustrates this proposition, being there held that the spreading of rumors with intent to enhance the price of hops, in the hearing of hop-planters, dealers and others, that the stock of hops was nearly exhausted, and that there would be a scarcity of hops, with intent to induce them not to bring their hops to market for a long time, and thereby greatly to enhance the price, constituted the offence of "ingrossing" (engrossing), at common law, notwithstanding the repeal of 5 & 6 Edw. & VI. c. 14 by 12 Geo. III. c. 76. Although this case, has been severely criticized, it has not, it seems, been directly overruled. And, as we have intimated, the general rule has been extended to embrace combinations or conspiracies to affect the price or market for stocks and government securities.

This was held in the celebrated case of the King *vs.* De Berenger and others. In that case De Berenger and seven others were tried and convicted of conspiracy in disseminating false reports and rumors that a peace would soon be made between England and France, and that Napoleon Bonaparte was dead, thereby attempting to occasion, without any just cause, a great increase and rise of the public government funds and securities, to the injury and damage of the subjects of the king, who should, on a certain day, purchase and buy such securities. The defendants moved an arrest of judgment upon several grounds; that no crime known to the law had been committed; that no adjudged case of conspiracy had gone as far as this; and that, if it were not a crime in itself to raise the price of government funds, a conspriracy to do so would not be illegal unless some collateral objects were stated to give it a criminal character.

Lord Ellenborough, in an opinion, the doctrine of which was endorsed by all of the judges, overruled all of the grounds relied on, holding that the conspriracy was by false rumors to raise the public funds and securities. The crime lay in the act of conspriacy and combination to effect that purpose, and it would have been complete although it had not been pursued to its consequences, or the parties had not been able to carry it into effect.

The purpose of such a conspiracy is itself mischievous, as it strikes at the price of a vendible commodity in the market, and, if it gives a fictitious price by means of false rumors, it is a fraud levelled against all the public, being against all such as may possibly have anything to do with the funds on that particular day. While the raising or lowering of the public funds is not per se a crime—for a man may have occasion to sell out a large sum, which may have the effect of depressing the price of stocks, or may buy in a large sum and thereby raise that price on a particular day—yet the conspiracy by a number of persons to raise the funds on a particular day is an offense prejudicial to a certain class of subjects.

A conspiracy to depress the stock of the Brooklyn Rapid Transit Company, dealt in an the Stock Exchange, is a conspiracy to injure trade or commerce. (People *vs.* Goslin, 73 N. Y.)

In 1874 the Legislature of the State of New York (Laws, 1874, ch. 440) passed a very stringent law against persons circulating rumors to affect the stock market, as follows:

"Sec. I. Every person who shall knowingly circulate false intelligence with intent of depreciating or advancing the market price of the public funds of the United States, or of any state or territory thereof, or of any foreign country or government, or the stocks, bonds, or evidence of debt of any corporation or association, or the market price of any merchandise or commodity whatever, shall be deemed guilty of a misdemeanor, and shall be punished upon conviction thereof, by a fine of not exceeding five thousand dollars, and imprisonment for a period not exceeding three years, or either.

"Sec. II. Every person who shall forge the name of any person, or the officer of any corporation, to any letter, message, or paper whatever with intent to advance or depreciate the market price of the public funds of the United States, or of any State or Territory thereof, or of any foreign country or government, or the market price of bonds or stock, or their evidence of debt issued by any corporation or association, or the market price of gold or silver coin or bullion, or of any merchandise or commodity whatever, shall, upon conviction, be adjudged guilty of forgery in the third degree, and shall be punished by imprisonment in a state prison for a term not exceeding five years."

This statute was repealed by L. 1886, ch. 593, Par. 1, subd. 94. Its provisions have been substantially re-enacted in the Penal Code, Par. 435. An indictment under this section charged the defendants with conspiring to occasion a fall in the market price of the stock of a corporation by "contriving, propagating and spreading" false rumors concerning its nancial condition, well knowing the same to be false, held that the indictment was sufficient, as the words "contriving and spreading" were the full equivalent of the statutory word "circulating," and motive, intent and guilty knowledge were also sufficiently charged. The defendants had published advertisements in New York newspapers to the effect that the stock of the corporation would fall, that it be obliged, under a decision of the court, to pay a heavy tax under the Ford act, and that it was going into the hands of a receiver, and it was held that the evidence was sufficient to sustain a conviction for having violated the provisions of this section, subd. 3.

In the State of New York the Supreme Court has decided that the law will not aid either party to enforce an agreement entered into for the purpose of advancing the selling price of stocks by means of ctitious dealings designed to produce a false impession on the minds of observers concerning their real value, and in that way to induce them to invest their money in such stocks. Such an agreement is void and against public policy. (Livermore vs. Bushnell, 5 Hun, 285. The court cited Thompson vs. Davies, 13, Johns, 112;

Brisbane *vs.* Adams, 3 Comst., 129; Hooker *vs.* Vande-
water, 4 Denio, 349; Stanton *vs.* Allen, 5 *id.* 434;
Marsh *vs.* Russel, 2 Lans., 340; 340.)

The practice of the London market in the flotation of
New shares on the Exchange is of interest. A "Special
Settlement" is provided for under Rule 138 of the Lon-
don Stock Exchange, as follows:

> The Secretary of the Share and Loan Department
> shall give three days' public notice of any application
> for a Special Settling day in the Shares or othe Se-
> curties of a new Company previously to such appli-
> cation being submitted to the Committee, who will ap-
> point a Special Settling-day provided that sufficient
> Certificates or Scrip are ready for delivery.

> The Committee will not fix a Special Settling-day
> for bargains in Shares or Securities issued to the
> Vendors, credited as fully or partly paid, until six
> months after the date fixed for the Special Settle-
> ment in the Shares or Securities subscribed for by
> the public, but this does not necessarily apply to re-
> organizatons or amalgamations of existing Companies,
> or to cases where no Public Shares are issued, or to
> cases where the Vendors take the whole of the shares
> issued for cash.

The English courts have frequently distinguished between legitimate and illegitimate manipulation in connection with these Special Settlements. The following
coment is from Poley and Gould, in "The History, Law
and Practice of the Stock Exchange" (London, 1907) p.
70:

> In making a market with a view to obtaining a
> Stock Exchange quotation, the method usually em-
> ployed is for the promoter to make a market through

the agency of brokers and jobbers—the brokers bidding for the shares at a premium until such time as sufficient shares have been applied for by the public, the jobbers looking to obtain an allottment. he operation ocasionally results in a loss, as the jobbers require to be indemnified, this is made good by the promoter.

The legality of making an articial market in this way was tested in the cases of Scott *v.* Brown and others, and Slaughter and May *v.* Brown and others 1892, 2 Q. B., 724). There the defendants, a firm of stockbrokers were brokers to the Company called the Steam Loop Company, Limited. The defendants had previously to the issue of the prospectus underwritten a portion of the share capital of the company, and were also holders of a number of shares. The plaintiff Scott was a promoter of the Company and interested in it; the other plaintiffs were solicitors to the company. Both plaintiffs instructed the defendants to purchase shares in the company, and these they had paid for. The cause of action arose from the defendants transferring their own shares to them. The evidence consisted of numbers of letters and telegrams from which it appeared that the plaintiff had been engaged, in pursuance to an agreement with one of the defendants, in purchasing shares at a premium with the object of inducing the public to believe that there was a real market for the shares. On hearing the evidence of the plaintiffs the Court of Appeals intimated that it appeared to disclose a criminal conspiracy of which they thought they ought to take judicial notice, and subsequently they delivered judgment.

In the course of his judgment Lindley, L. H., said: "In this case the correspondence put in evidence by the plaintiff in support of the claim he made at the trial shows conclusively that the sole object of the plaintiff in ordering shares to be bought for him at a

premium was to impose upon and to deceive the public by leading the public to suppose that there were
buyers of such shares at a premium on the Stock
Exchange when in fact there were nothing but himself. he plaintiff's purchase was an actual purchase,
not a sham purchase. That is true, but is also true
that the sole object of the purchase was to cheat and
mislead the public. Under these circumstances the
plaintiff must look elsewhere than to a court of justice for such assistance as he may require against the
persons he employed to assist him in his fraud. If
the claim to such assistance is based on his illegalcon-
tract, any rights which he may have, irrespective of
his illegal contract will, of course, be recognized and
enforced. But his illegal contract confers no rights
on him (See Pearce *v.* Brooks, L. R. 1. Ex. 213).
The illegal purposes of the plaintiff distinguishes this
case from Wetherell *v.* Jones (3 B. and Ad. 221) and
others of a similar kind. I am quite aware that what
the plaintiff has done is very commonly done; it is
done every day. But this is immaterial. Picking
pockets and various forms of cheating are common
enough, and are nevertheless illegal."

Charles Duguid (of the London *Morning Post*), in
"The Stock Exchange" (London, 1904), p. 147:

On the Stock Exchange practice of making a market, a couple of important judgments were delivered in
1892. In the course of one of them Mr. Justice
Wright remarked that "if persons for their own purposes of speculation create an artificial price in the
market by transactions which are not real, but are
made at a nominal premium merely for the purpose
of inducing the public to take shares, they are guilty

of as gross a fraud as has ever been committed and of a fraud that can be criminally brought home to them."

An admirable discussion of the question, "Should Speculation be Regulated by Law" by Professor Emery is to be found in the *Journal of Accountancy* (April, 1908). Professor Emery argues:

Speculation in securities is bound up in the closest way with the whole matter of the investment of capital and the accumulating of the necessary means for carrying out great industrial enterprises. Just in so far as the stock market has a speculative clientele. it becomes an open and broad market and facilitates the disposal of great issues of stocks and bonds which are necessary for carrying out for the industrial undertakings of the present age.

The limitation of this broad market must invariably prove a hindrance in the financing of the most legitimate enterprises, and any interference with the freedom of speculation must inveitably lessen openness of the market. If we attempt to secure the benefits, while restricting the evils of speculation, through discriminating against certain kinds of transactions, we find it impossible to really discriminate in any way according to the form of the transactions, while, inevitably, by restricting the forms of commerce and of commercial methods, we put a severe handicap upon entirely legitimate enterprise. There is only one way in which speculation can be stopped altogether, and that is by giving up the system of private property and adopting the Socialistic state.

It will be seen then that speculation s not a product of stock and produce exchanges. Speculation existed long before them, and it was only when speculation from natural causes became more and more important that men engaged chiefly in speculative trade formed organizations in order to adopt a general system of rules for the conduct of such business.

The real cause then of the modern exchange in modern speculation is to be found, so far as commodities are concerned, in the marvelous improvements in the method of transportation and communication which have made the market for staple commodities a world market, in which prices are determined by the condition of supply and demand of many different sections separated by thousands of miles.

So far as speculation in stocks is concerned this has been the inevitable result of the enormous multiplication of securities, due to the extension of corporate methods to business, which in itself is the result of huge modern enterprises demanding contributions of capital from a large number of small investors. The material progress of the last half century would have been impossible without such investment. Such investment would have been impossible without the multiplication of such securities inevitably brings about speculation.

Speculation, even on the part of the public, with all its evils, has a very important beneficial effect. Unless the public speculates to some extent the market will not only be very restricted but will be in consequence much more open to manipulation. The bigger and broader the market the less chances there are for rigging prices. It may seem a very high price to pay for the open market that the speculative spirit should continue on the part of the public, but it would be a mistake to suppose that speculation can be confined to a few great operators and still offer the benefits which the present market gives.

From a study of the effects of speculation and the effects of all suggested methods of controlling it, the conclusion is almost irresistible; that legitimate and illegitimate transactions are so closely bound together, and the whole business of speculation is so closely connected with the interests of actual commerce, that any interference with the delicate machinery by the blundering fingers of the law will diminish the beneficial elements of speculation without effectively diminishing its evils.